BE AN ENCOURAGER, NOT A DISCOURAGER!

Ralph Gonzales

BE AN ENCOURAGER, NOT A DISCOURAGER!
Copyright © 2018 Ralph Gonzales

Book Cover Designed by Truth Design and Photography
ISBN: 9781718066588

TABLE OF CONTENTS

Chapter 1

BE AN ENCOURAGER, NOT A DISCOURAGER!

And we urge you, brothers and sisters, warn those who are idle and disruptive, encourage the disheartened, help the weak, be patient with everyone.

(1 Thessalonians 5:14; NIV)

In this small book, I want to show you how powerful encouragement is in the life of any person, but especially, a new believer in Christ. As Paul wrote to Timothy, "Preach the word; be prepared in season and out of season; correct, rebuke and **encourage** with great patience and careful instruction" (2 Timothy 4:2; NIV).

In this verse, *encourage* (or exhort) is "a term referring to encouragement or urging. This is from the Greek term *parakaleson*, which involves support, comfort, and aid."[1]

1

Encourage means: "To inspire with courage, spirit, or confidence: His coach encouraged him throughout the marathon race to keep running."[2]

That's what encouragers do! They encourage you to finish the race, especially during the hard times. As John C. Maxwell writes,

An experiment was conducted years ago to measure people's capacity to endure pain. Psychologists measured how long a barefooted person could stand in a bucket of ice water. They found that one factor made it possible for some people to stand in the ice water twice as long as others. Can you guess what that factor was? It was encouragement. When another person was present, giving support and encouragement, the sufferers were able to endure the pain much longer than their unencouraged counterparts.[3]

Encouraging others is a powerful thing! Maxwell goes on to write,

Lack of encouragement can hinder a person from living a healthy, productive life. But when a person feels encouraged, he can face the impossible and overcome incredible adversity. And the person who gives the gift of encouragement becomes an influencer in his life.[4]

Be an Encourager!

As believers in Christ, we need to learn to be encouragers—not discouragers—to our brothers and sisters-in-Christ. This is vital because those around us will make many mistakes. If they don't have someone there to pick them up when they're feeling down, they may stay down and never get up to finish the race. So, when they come to us to confess their sins and talk about their struggles, we need to refrain from saying condemning phrases like, **"HOW COULD YOU DO THAT?"** or **"YOU'RE NO CHRISTIAN!"** This is especially true if they are new converts. Condemning phrases are not going to help anyone!

You must understand that before they even came to us, they were already beating themselves up; thinking they are a failure. Of course, you know the devil is also right there to convince them that they are a failure as well. When people fall into sin or mess up, they go through major mind battles whether or not they should even tell us what they did. They have thoughts like, *"what is he/she going to think if I open up?" "They may kick me out of the church if I tell them what I did." "I don't want to tell them, all they're going to do is condemn me."* If we're honest with ourselves, we've had thoughts like these go through our minds as well before we told a leader about where we've fallen short.

So, the last thing we need to do is sit in judgment of their sin and put them down. Think about it; they're coming to us for help, encouragement, and direction. Don't kick them when they are down; instead, be like the Holy Spirit and try to lead them back to the heart of God. When we sin or mess up, the Holy Spirit is there to convict and show us where we missed it. In love, He tells us, *"All you have to do is ask for forgiveness, repent (turn from it), don't do it anymore, and go forward."* That's what we need to do too.

For example, let's say someone comes to you and is feeling terrible because they slipped and said a cuss word when they got angry. Or maybe they fell into sin and masturbated, watched porn, or fornicated. Perhaps they went out drinking or got high. These are all things that, unfortunately, some new converts fall into during their process of getting delivered from the bondages and addictions in their lives. Now, I want to make something explicit; none of the things mentioned here are okay for anyone to do. They are sinful, and if a person continues to persist in doing these things, they could end up in hell.

> Don't you realize that those who do wrong will not inherit the Kingdom of God? Don't fool yourselves. Those

who indulge in sexual sin, or who worship idols, or commit adultery, or are male prostitutes, or practice homosexuality, or are thieves, or greedy people, or drunkards, or are abusive, or cheat people—none of these will inherit the Kingdom of God. Some of you were once like that. But you were cleansed; you were made holy; you were made right with God by calling on the name of the Lord Jesus Christ and by the Spirit of our God (1 Corinthians 6:9-11; NLT).

But as believers in Christ, we must speak the truth in love to them (Ephesians 4:15) about what they did and call sin what it is— sin. We need to tell them of their need to ask God for forgiveness, repent (turn from it), and move forward. But don't be harsh with them. Instead, encourage them with Scripture. 1 John 1:9 says, *"If we confess our sins, He is faithful and just to forgive us our sins and to cleanse us from all unrighteousness."* Tell them, *"It's good that you feel bad about the sin you committed because I would be scared for you if you didn't. So, get up and go forward."* Be an encourager. Make sure you pray with them and check in on them regularly. Teach them about Jesus' delivering power and share with them how the Lord freed you from different things. Help them through the process of getting delivered. For some, deliverance happens instantly, but others may struggle and fall a few times before they are totally set free (Proverbs 24:16). **This is what it means to be there one for another! You must get your hands dirty!**

You see, encouragers don't look at a person's past. Rather, encouragers look at the potential future of the person. They speak about a better day coming and don't condemn people when they mess up or call them devils. They correct, direct, and encourage them to move forward. This is how we must be with our brothers and sisters when they fall into sin or come to us with their shortcomings.

In Galatians 6:1-3, Paul wrote, "Brethren, if a man is overtaken in any trespass, you who are spiritual restore such a one in a spirit of gentleness, considering yourself lest you also be tempted. Bear one another's burdens, and so fulfill the law of Christ. For if anyone thinks himself to be something, when he is nothing, he deceives himself." This passage teaches us how to **respond** in our dealings with those who fall into sin and come to us with their sins. Our reactions to them reveal a lot of where we're at spiritually. Notice it says, "Brethren, if a man is overtaken in any trespass, **you who are spiritual restore** such a one in a spirit of gentleness…." Keep these words in mind! We are to focus on being *restorers,* not *destroyers*!

One problem I see with a lot of believers is that after they have been saved for a while, they tend to forget that they have been delivered from a few things themselves. They overlook how much grace and patience God and others had with them when they first got saved, and even now as they continue to fall short. At times, we tend to be harder on other believers and raise the bar higher for them than we would for ourselves. We expect them to be as spiritual as we are even though they're just babes in the Lord, even though we are more mature in our faith. We expect them to have the same convictions and discipline as us in every area of their lives overnight. That's unfair and wrong! Listen to me; they will get to where you're spiritually **IF** you will encourage them and be willing to help them grow in Christ.

The reason people are harsh with others is, again, because they forget about how much grace and patience the Lord and others had with them when they first got saved. Some act this way because they're full of pride, others because they're on a power trip. I feel sorry for anyone who has to deal with believers on a power trip. Listen to me, be realistic with those who come to you with their struggles. I didn't say *compromise*—I said to *be realistic*. Speak to them the things that are realistic for where they're at spiritually.

It would be unfair and unrealistic for me to expect my son, Sammy, who just started learning how to read and write, to do high school assignments simply because I know he can read and write. He won't be able to do that level of work until he's mature enough and has acquired the necessary knowledge to handle such assignments. The same is true with young believers. They will not be at the same level as you spiritually overnight, but as you encourage them, **OVER TIME,** they'll get to where they need to be eventually.

If we want God to extend mercy and grace to us when we mess up, we must extend it to others. Recall the words of Jesus, "Do not judge others, and you will not be judged. For you will be treated as you treat others. The standard you use in judging is the standard by which you will be judged" (Matthew 7:1-2; NLT). If we don't extend mercy and grace to others, we can't expect it from the Lord. The thing that helps me to be patient and extend love to others is to remember how patient, merciful, and graceful the Lord has been with me.

The point I'm trying to make is that spiritual growth takes time. During that time, new believers will make a lot of mistakes, and they need us to pick them up, not tear them down. How we deal with them could be the factor that determines if they will continue to serve God or whether or not they will fulfill their callings. How we deal with people affects their eternity!

Be Approachable

Let me also express the importance of being approachable. If you are not approachable, or if those around you don't feel you're approachable, you can hinder others from being healed and delivered. How can I make this statement? James 5:16 (NIV) specifically says, "Therefore confess your sins to each other and pray for each other so that you may be healed." It is vital to the growth of a young believer to confess his/her sins to God (1 John 1:9) and to another; preferably to a leader (James 5:16). Why? Because **we're only as sick as our secrets.** When a person can tell someone else about the wrong they did, it puts it out in the open, and there's a release that takes place, which leads to freedom. But for many, this freedom may not be able to take place because they feel their leadership is not approachable.

The way we become approachable to those around us is through building a relationship with them. Show love and concern and reach out to them on a regular basis. If we do these things, people will come to us with their deepest struggles, thereby opening the door for us to start discipling them.

Hard times will come to young believers. They will face moments when they feel like giving up. Moments of worrying, or doubting; when they hurt, have marital problems, endure guilt for falling short, and fall prey to attacks from Satan. It's then that they need you to be an *encourager*, not a *discourager*. As you will see in the next chapter, it will help them to keep going forward.

Chapter 2

BARNABAS, "SON OF ENCOURAGEMENT"

Finally, brothers and sisters, rejoice! Strive for full restoration,
encourage one another, be of one mind, live in peace. And the
God of love and peace will be with you.
(2 Corinthians 13:11; NIV)

I want to shift my focus now to the lives of John called Mark, Barnabas, and the apostle Paul. The first person I want to look at is Barnabas. You first read about him in Acts 4:32-37 (NIV):

All the believers were one in heart and mind. No one claimed that any of their possessions was their own, but they shared everything they had. [33] With great power the apostles continued to testify to the resurrection of the Lord Jesus. And God's grace was so powerfully at work in them all [34] that there were no needy persons among them. For from time to time those who owned land or houses sold them, brought the money from the sales [35] and put it at the apostles' feet, and it was distributed to anyone who had need. [36] Joseph, a Levite from Cyprus, whom the apostles called Barnabas (which means "son of encouragement"), [37] sold a field he owned and brought the money and put it at the apostles' feet.

These verses show us the kind of man Barnabas was. He was willing to sell his property and lay the money from the sale at the apostles' feet for the sake of the brethren. This act reveals he had a heart for people and truly wanted to see their needs met.

Notice also he was named Barnabas (which is translated *son of encouragement*) by the apostles. This means he must have been a man who was always encouraging those around him. I want to say again; the apostles named him that! It wasn't a self-proclaimed name.

Let me ask you, if the leaders in your church named you, what would they call you? Likewise, what have others labeled you? Have you been called names such as big mouth, prideful, gossip, clown, selfish, loving, compassionate, kind, or encourager? Whatever you have been labeled, there is some truth to it; whether you like it or not. It's the reputation you've built by the actions you have taken. Now, if you don't like the label on your life, then I suppose you need to make some changes.

Before I got saved, I was labeled a thug, a gang member, a liar, a player (which were all true), and many more negative things. But after giving my life to Christ, I'm now known as a child of God, a pastor, a man of integrity, a loving person, and many more positive things! This is all because I gave my life to Christ and made some changes.

Barnabas and Saul

Barnabas was always encouraging those around him. For instance, God used Barnabas during the early years to encourage Saul in his walk with God. Around three years after Saul's dramatic conversion, he went up to Jerusalem (Galatians 1:15-18) and was rejected by the disciples of the church there when he tried to join them. It was then that God used Barnabas to convince the apostles that Saul—who is called Paul—was really saved and a disciple of Jesus Christ.

> And when Saul had come to Jerusalem, he tried to join the disciples; but they were all afraid of him, and did not believe that he was a disciple. [27] But Barnabas took him and brought him to the apostles. And he declared to them how he had seen the Lord on the road, and that He had spoken to him, and how he had preached boldly at

Damascus in the name of Jesus. [28] So he was with them at Jerusalem, coming in and going out (Acts 9:26-28).

While he was still known as Saul, Paul had a terrible reputation with the Christians. He was the "biggest" persecutor of the early church. He writes in Galatians 1:13, "For you have heard of my former conduct in Judaism, how I persecuted the church of God beyond measure and tried to destroy it." Acts 8:3 says, "As for Saul, he made havoc of the church, entering every house, and dragging off men and women, committing them to prison."

This man was known and feared by the church because of how vehemently he was persecuting them. As we read in Acts 9:26b, "...he tried to join the disciples, but they were **all afraid** of him and did not believe that he was a disciple." When he tried to join them, I'm sure they were thinking things like, *"Yeah right!" "You're not saved!" "I don't believe you gave your life to Christ!" "You came here to drag us off to prison like you did with our brothers and sisters in the Lord!"*

People did not believe he was saved, which means people did not trust him or his words due to his reputation. This could have been hurtful and offensive, even enough to make him not want to serve God or perhaps even want nothing to do with the believers in Jerusalem. But as the text makes clear, Saul wasn't offended by their initial rejection of him and decided to meet with the apostles.

It resulted in him staying with them for a short time in Jerusalem, *coming in and going out* (Acts 9:28). This was because Barnabas (son of encouragement) became the bridge between Saul and the apostles.

We need more people to be like Barnabas in the church. When those with messed up pasts or bad reputations walk into our churches, someone needs to be there to come alongside them, love them, speak life to them, disciple them, and introduce them to other believers. I don't doubt that Barnabas was probably praying for Paul (Saul) when he was persecuting the churches because that's what Jesus taught believers to do:

> "You have heard that it was said, 'You shall love your neighbor and hate your enemy.' [44] But I say to you, love your enemies, bless those who curse you, do good to those who hate you, and pray for those who spitefully use you and persecute you" (Matthew 5:43-44).

Nobody persecuted the church more than Saul. When Paul came to Barnabas and told him the testimony of how the Lord appeared to him, and how he had been preaching in Damascus, Barnabas must have thought, *"Praise God! This is an answer to prayer!"*

Barnabas believed that Saul was really saved, and he believed Saul's testimony about the Lord appearing to him. That's why when Barnabas brought him to the apostles, he declared to them Saul's testimony of salvation and how he preached boldly in Damascus (Acts 9:27). Barnabas became the bridge between Saul and the apostles. He was the one who convinced the apostles that their former enemy was now a believer in Christ. The apostles would then, in turn, convince the church of the same.

Saul Was Sent to Tarsus

[29] And he spoke boldly in the name of the Lord Jesus and disputed against the Hellenists, but they attempted to kill him. [30] When the brethren found out, they brought him down to Caesarea and sent him out to Tarsus (Acts 9:29-30).

After a short time with the church in Jerusalem, Saul was sent to Tarsus for his own protection. As you read on, you see that he stayed there for several years before Barnabas sought him and brought him to Antioch to help the church there.

Now those who were scattered after the persecution that arose over Stephen traveled as far as Phoenicia, Cyprus, and Antioch, preaching the word to no one but the Jews only. [20] But some of them were men from Cyprus and Cyrene, who, when they had come to Antioch, spoke to the Hellenists, preaching the Lord Jesus. [21] And the hand of the Lord was with them, and a great number believed and turned to the Lord. [22] Then news of these things came to the ears of the church in Jerusalem, and they sent out Barnabas to go as far as Antioch. [23] When he came and had seen the grace of God, he was glad, and encouraged them all that with purpose of heart they should continue with the Lord.[24] For he was a good man, full of the Holy Spirit and of faith. And a great many people were added to the Lord. [25] Then Barnabas departed for Tarsus to seek Saul. [26] And when he had found him, he brought him to Antioch. So it was that for a whole year they assembled with the church and taught a great many people. And the disciples were first called Christians in Antioch (Acts 11:19-26).

I want to first point out that Barnabas was sent as far as Antioch by the church in Jerusalem (Acts 11:22) because a great number of people turned to the Lord. Notice verse 23, "When he came and had seen the grace of God, he was glad, and **encouraged** them all…" After he "encouraged them all," the Scripture goes on to say that *"a great many people were added to the Lord"* (Acts 11:24). Herein lies the power of being an encourager, not a discourager.

Afterward, we see that Barnabas "departed for Tarsus to seek after Saul" (Acts 11:25). When Barnabas found Saul there, he brought Saul back to Antioch with him and "for a whole year they assembled with the church and taught a great many people" (Acts 11:26).

The offering from the Antioch church, for the Jerusalem church in a time of need, was sent by the hands of Barnabas and Saul.

> And in these days prophets came from Jerusalem to Antioch. [28] Then one of them, named Agabus, stood up and showed by the Spirit that there was going to be a great famine throughout all the world, which also happened in the days of Claudius Caesar. [29] Then the disciples, each according to his ability, determined to send relief to the brethren dwelling in Judea. [30] This they also did, and sent it to the elders by the hands of Barnabas and Saul (Acts 11:27-30).

> Agabus delivered his message to the Antioch believers, and they determined to help their fellow Christians in

Judea. The purpose of true prophecy is not to satisfy our curiosity about the future, but to stir up our hearts to do the will of God. The believers could not stop the famine from coming, but they could send relief to those in need.[5]

Once Barnabas and Saul's journey to bring famine relief to Jerusalem was complete, they returned to Antioch with Mark accompanying them.

> And Barnabas and Saul returned from Jerusalem when they had fulfilled their ministry, and they also took with them John whose surname was Mark (Acts 12:25).

Then, in Acts 13, a word from the Holy Spirit came forth for Barnabas and Saul as certain prophets and teachers were ministering to the Lord.

> Now in the church that was at Antioch there were certain prophets and teachers: Barnabas, Simeon who was called Niger, Lucius of Cyrene, Manaen who had been brought up with Herod the tetrarch, and Saul.[2] As they ministered to the Lord and fasted, the Holy Spirit said, "Now separate to Me Barnabas and Saul for the work to

which I have called them." [3] Then, having fasted and prayed, and laid hands on them, they sent them away. [4] So, being sent out by the Holy Spirit, they went down to Seleucia, and from there they sailed to Cyprus. [5] And when they arrived in Salamis, they preached the word of God in the synagogues of the Jews. They also had John as their assistant (Acts 13:1-5).

This was the beginning of Saul's first missionary journey. Notice that God had Barnabas with him.

John called Mark and Barnabas

Another person that joined them on their first mission trip was **John, called Mark.** "And when they arrived in Salamis, they preached the word of God in the synagogues of the Jews. They also had John as their assistant" (Acts 13:5).

Barnabas and Paul took John Mark with them *as their assistant.* He was a cousin to Barnabas (Colossians 4:10), and his mother's house in Jerusalem was a gathering place for believers (Acts 12:12). Most believe it was Peter who led John Mark to faith in Christ (1 Peter 5:13). After this, they went through the island of Paphos and were used powerfully by God there (Acts 13:6-12). What happens next is made clear in Acts 13:13, "Now when Paul and his party set sail from Paphos, they came to Perga in

Pamphylia; and **John, departing from them, returned to Jerusalem.**"

The Bible isn't clear why John departed from Paul and Barnabas. Some speculate that it may have been because of a lack of courage or commitment. Perhaps he could have been home-sick since we know from Acts 12 that his mother lived in Jerusalem. Whatever the motive was behind his leaving, the point is that he left.

The following is an overview of what took place next from **Acts 13:13-15:35:**

- **Acts 13:13-52:** By ship, Saul and his associate went to Perga in the province of Pamphylia, where John Mark left and returned to Jerusalem. From here, they went to Pisidian Antioch in the Roman province of Galatia, where Saul preached the gospel in the synagogue there. On a Sabbath, Saul explained that the people of Jerusalem and their rulers did not recognize Jesus, but that God raised Him from the dead; he cites Ps 2:7, Isa 55:3, and Ps 16:10 as fulfilled in Jesus. On the next Sabbath, Paul and Barnabas warned the Jews, who have rejected their message, that they will take the gospel to the Gentiles, citing Isa

49:6 as predictive of this. Paul and Barnabas were forced by the Jews to leave Antioch.

- **Acts 14:1-20:** From Antioch, Paul and Barnabas went to Iconium, where they also preached in the synagogue and were forced to leave. They then traveled to Lystra and Derbe, cities of Lycaonia. In Lystra, because of Paul's healing of a lame man, the people presumed Barnabas and Paul as gods. But Jews from Antioch and Iconium convinced the crowds otherwise, and they stoned Paul.

- **Acts 14:20-28:** Paul and Barnabas traced their steps backward, traveled through the cities in which they already preached the gospel and returned to Antioch in Syria.[6]

- **Acts 15:1-35:** Jews from Judea taught that circumcision is necessary for Christians. Paul and Barnabas disputed this. A council in Jerusalem debated the issue, and letters were sent to the churches of Antioch, Syria, and Cilicia, saying that circumcision is not necessary, but only abstinence from idolatry, blood, things strangled, and sexual immorality. Judas and Silas served as visiting ministers in Antioch with Paul and Barnabas.[7]

God always does things for a purpose. I believe that God intended for Barnabas to accompany Saul in his early years as a believer and during his first missionary journey because Barnabas was an encourager. Remember from the previous chapter that the word, "encourage," means "to inspire with hope, courage, or confidence."

In all the ministry work they did together, I believe that Barnabas was meant to be there with Saul, especially for the hard times that Saul endured. We don't know for sure, but this is a reasonable assumption, given the kind of man Barnabas was.

The Big Split

Paul and Barnabas also remained in Antioch, teaching and preaching the word of the Lord, with many others also. [36] Then after some days, Paul said to Barnabas, "Let us now go back and visit our brethren in every city where we have preached the word of the Lord, and see how they are doing." [37] Now Barnabas was determined to take with them John called Mark. [38] But Paul insisted that they should not take with them the one who had departed from them in Pamphylia, and had not gone with them to the work. [39] Then the contention became so sharp that they parted from one another. And so Barnabas took Mark and sailed to Cyprus; [40] but Paul chose Silas and departed, being commended by the brethren to the grace of God. [41] And he went through Syria and Cilicia, strengthening the churches (Acts 15:35-41).

As these verses explained, Paul did not want (John) Mark to accompany them on this journey. Whatever reason he left them, it was enough grounds for Paul not to want him to go along with them any further. When this separation took place, Paul must have forgotten how God used Barnabas in his life during his early years when the disciples in the church in Jerusalem rejected him.

Now, before he came back to them, Mark obviously had to deal with many thoughts and feelings. Maybe some feelings of shame, guilt, or embarrassment. Perhaps thoughts may have gone through his head like, *"What is Paul going to think and say to me when I see him?"* It probably wasn't the easiest thing to do to come back after already leaving. Tradition says that Mark repented and asked to go along with them on their second journey to the north and was ready to serve once he got there. But as we read, Paul rejected him.

At this point in Mark's life, after being rejected by his leader (Paul), he may have felt hurt, unwanted, or possibly angry and even offended. He must have had a million thoughts going through his mind; thoughts of possibly wanting to go back to Jerusalem again, or maybe that Paul is rude and unforgiving. Put yourself in his shoes and think about how you would have felt. Think about how you felt the last time you were willing to do something for a leader in your life, a loved one, and were rejected by them. It didn't feel so good, did it? NO! You were probably crushed on the inside. You were probably mad and offended. Maybe you even thought something like, "*I didn't want to help anyway!*"

Now, as if being rejected by Paul wasn't enough, Acts 15:39 tells us Paul and Barnabas had such a sharp disagreement about Mark that they split up and parted company. When this happened, Mark must have felt terrible and responsible for the break-up. Imagine how he must've felt at that point. Just imagine how you would have felt.

Mark came back after dealing with his feelings of being ashamed for leaving. But when he came back, he was rejected by his leader, Paul. Then still, he's the reason Barnabas and Paul decided to part ways. You know he felt terrible! Maybe he had thoughts going through his mind to just give up or go back home. And of course, you know the devil was right there playing all kinds of mind games with him. *"You should have never come back." "Look what you did!"* This would have been enough for anyone to want to give up and go back home.

Even though there was a difference of opinion between Paul and Barnabas about Mark, God turned this situation around for the good. Instead of *one* missionary team, there were now *two*. Scripture teaches that after this took place, "Barnabas took Mark and sailed to Cyprus; but Paul chose Silas and departed...And he went through Syria and Cilicia" (Acts 15:39-41).

Barnabas and Mark

History tells us that when Barnabas and Mark went to Cyprus, Mark preached boldly. I believe that was a direct result of Barnabas being an encourager to Mark, not a discourager.

As time went on, it is clear from Paul's letters that he grew to respect Mark. Paul writes in Colossians 4:10, "Aristarchus my fellow prisoner greets you, with **Mark** the cousin of Barnabas (about whom you received instructions: if he comes to you, **welcome him**)." He wrote elsewhere in 2 Timothy 4:11, "Only Luke is with me. Get **Mark** and bring him with you, **for he is useful to me for ministry**." These verses make it clear that Mark redeemed his reputation with Paul. Paul now recognized Mark's sincerity and his value as a minister of the Lord Jesus Christ. Clearly, this shows us that these men didn't hold on to grudges, but allowed the past to be the past.

When you're in the ministry long enough, problems will occur. Differences will take place between you and your brothers and sisters; the best thing to do when they occur (because they will happen), is to be quick to forgive and not hold on to grudges.

25

Unforgiveness will only keep you divided and separated from your brothers and sisters with whom the Lord intends you to labor.

Also, it must be noted, the apostle Paul writes about Barnabas a few years after their split in 1 Corinthians 9:6: "Or *is it* only Barnabas and I *who* have no right to refrain from working?" Most believe that Paul's reference here to Barnabas indicates that their separation had not caused a complete break in their relationship. Barnabas is mentioned because he along with Paul had worked in a trade during the course of their ministry.[8]

The book, *Jesus Freaks Vol. 2*, recounts what took place after all this:

"John Mark eventually traveled with Peter and, at the request of the church in Rome, wrote the gospel of Mark from Peter's teachings. Peter endorsed the writings and had them distributed to the churches for the encouragement and education of their growing congregations.

Peter later sent John Mark into Egypt and Africa as a missionary. He traveled throughout Lybia, Marmorica, Ammonica, and Pentapolis (northern African prefectures above the Sahara), preaching and teaching wherever he could. Finally, he established and shepherded a church in Alexandria, Egypt, where he stayed for several years. Mark's teaching that all people are free in Christ by accepting Jesus as their Lord and Savior had begun to transform the community there. The local heathen priests began to lose business and were so pricked in their hearts by his preaching that they began to loathe him. It was not long before they were plotting to kill him.

It is recorded that on the twenty-first day of April, A.D. 64, in the eighth year of Nero's reign as emperor, Mark preached a sermon remembering Jesus' suffering on the cross and resurrection from the dead as his Easter Sunday sermon. The local heathen priest chose this day to rouse as many as possible against Mark and see that he never preached again.

With a large crowd, they stormed the church with huge hooks and ropes, overpowering those in the congregation, and seized John Mark. Tying him with the rope and snagging and jabbing him with hooks, they dragged him through the congregation, through the streets of the town, and out of the city, leaving a trail of blood and flesh in the gospel writer's wake. By the time he was outside of the town, there was not one place on Mark's body from which blood did not flow.

John Mark commended his spirit into the hands of his Lord and died. Yet his death was not enough for the enraged crowd. The priest wanted to desecrate his body so badly that it could not be buried. They called for fire to be built to burn the body, but a sudden and mysterious storm arose that scattered the crowd. John Mark's body was deserted on the spot where he had died.

In the excitement of the storm, members of his congregation came and reclaimed Mark's corpse. When things had calmed down some time later, they gave his body a proper and respectful burial." [9]

As we see, after being rejected and the subject of the breakup between Barnabas and Paul, Mark went on to do great things for God. The results of Mark's life are directly connected to Barnabas not giving up on him! He continued to encourage Mark to keep going forward. Barnabas hung in there with Mark through thick and thin. You can just imagine him telling Mark when he was down, *"You can do it" "Keep on pressing on!" "Don't give up!" "You can make it!" "God loves you and has a plan for your life!" "He's forgiven you of all your sins!" "Forget your past!" "Just move forward!"*

Be a Barnabas

There's so much power in encouraging people. Even though Mark had some failures in his Christian walk with God, Barnabas didn't give up on him. He continued to encourage him and speak life into him.

If it weren't for the encouragement of Barnabas (his cousin), I don't believe Mark would have done all that he did for the Kingdom of God. Those around you, especially new converts, need you to be a Barnabas to them. If we're not, they may not make it through the hard times they face, and thus, will not fulfill the callings on their lives.

Hard times will come to those around us. Just as we all have faced hard times, they will face seasons where they feel like giving up. Worries, doubts, hurt, marital problems, guilt for falling short, and attacks from Satan are inevitable. Its then, in those times, that they need us to be a Barnabas; an *encourager*, not a *discourager*, to them.

Barnabas wasn't the one who would look for fault in a person to condemn them. He was someone who looked for the good in a person and spoke life and hope into them. In a way, you can say Barnabas was like a cheerleader. Why? Because cheerleaders *cheer* for their team whether they're winning or losing. They even cheer when they're being blown out! In the same way, Barnabas cheered people on whether they were doing good or bad, and we need to do the same!

You see, encouragers don't look at the past of a person, but look at what their future can hold. They speak about a better day coming. They don't condemn people when they mess up and call them devils. They correct, direct, and encourage them to move forward. They remind them what 1 John 1:9 says, "That if we confess our sins He is faithful and just to forgive and cleanse us of all unrighteousness." This is what we must do.

Barnabas was drawn to People He Could Encourage

"As Barnabas' life shows, we are rarely in a situation where there isn't someone we can encourage. Our tendency however, is to criticize instead. It may be important at times to point out someone's shortcomings but before we have the right to do this we must build that person's trust through encouragement. Are you prepared to encourage those with whom you come in contact today?" [10]

Personal Application: Have you been an *encourager* or a *discourager* to your brothers and sisters in the Lord? You know the answer. Choose today to be a Barnabas to those around you. Choose to be an encourager, not a discourager. Be realistic with new converts, your brothers and sisters-in-Christ, and those you're discipling. When they fall short (and they will), correct, direct, and encourage them to move forward the way it is taught in this book. Speak words of a better future to them. Lastly, be approachable so that they not only confess their sins to God but also to you, so they can be healed.

NOTES

Chapter 1
1. "What does 2 Timothy 4:2 mean?" BibleRef, accessed June 19, 2018, https://www.bibleref.com/2-Timothy/4/2-Timothy-4-2.html.
2. "encourage," Dictionary.com, from Random House, Inc., accessed May 9, 2018, http://www.dictionary.com/browse/encourage.
3. Maxwell and Dornan, Becoming a Person of Influence, 47.
4. Maxwell and Dornan, Becoming a Person of Influence, 48.

Chapter 2
5. https://asucru.files.wordpress.com/2008/01/wiersbe-commentary-new-testament.pdfpg.360
6. http://www.mycrandall.ca/courses/ntintro/acts.htm
7. http://biblesummarybychapter.blogspot.com/2011/04/acts.html
8. Note on 1 Cor. 9:6, New Spirit-Filled Life Bible, NKJV, pg. 1591
9. Jesus Freaks: Jesus Freaks Vol. II: Stories of Revolutionaries Who Changed Their World Fearing God, Not Man by DC Talk (2002, Paperback)
10. Life Application Study Bible, NKJV, pg. 2007

ABOUT THE AUTHOR

Ralph Gonzales is the Senior Pastor of Praise Chapel Pittsburg and oversees Praise Chapel Bay Area Impact, a network of churches he has planted in Northern California and abroad. He and this network of churches are under the covering of Praise Chapel Global, a church multiplication movement in over thirty nations. He has authored several books, emphasizing on biblical discipleship and spiritual discipline. Also, he is the founder of Equipping the Saints Bible School. Ralph and his wife Wendi have been married for over 20 years and have six children together.

New Life

What's Next After Getting Saved?

Available at Amazon

Nueva Vida

¿Qué Sigue Después De Ser Salvo?

Available at Amazon

Available at Amazon

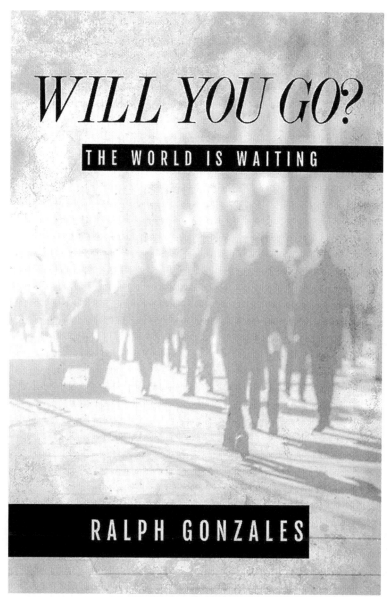

Available at Amazon

What's on Your Mind?

It affects everything!

Ralph Gonzales

Available at Amazon

SMALL GROUP

BIBLE STUDIES

Matthew 7:24-27

RALPH GONZALES

Available at Amazon

Be an Encourager, Not a Discourager!

Available at Amazon

40

Be an Encourager, Not a Discourager!

Available at Amazon

Made in the USA
Las Vegas, NV
23 March 2023

69513549R00028